# DEEPER SECRETS

If you had the good sense to get yourself a copy of *My Secret File* you'll know that it contained the absolute truth about the loves and hates of one of the world's greatest human beings . . . YOU!

Now you can let it all hang out about the rest of them. Adults can give you a great time or a hard time and usually you don't have much say in the matter anyway. So why not put it all down in this super-secret, sly, seditious scratch-pad – *Deeper Secrets*.

# DEEPER
# SECRETS

JOHN ASTROP

PUFFIN BOOKS

Puffin Books, Penguin Books Ltd, Harmondsworth, Middlesex, England
Penguin Books, 40 West 23rd Street, New York, New York 10010, U.S.A.
Penguin Books Australia Ltd, Ringwood, Victoria, Australia
Penguin Books Canada Ltd, 2801 John Street, Markham, Ontario, Canada L3R 1B4
Penguin Books (N.Z.) Ltd, 182–190 Wairau Road, Auckland 10, New Zealand

First published 1984

Filmset in Baskerville (Linotron 202) by
Rowland Phototypesetting Ltd, Bury St Edmunds, Suffolk
Made and printed in Great Britain by
Richard Clay (The Chaucer Press) Ltd, Bungay, Suffolk

# GERROFF!

*Deeper Secrets* are my positively private, personal and prohibited observations of the doings and happenings to the nice and nasty friends, relations and idiots that surround, control and exploit my precious life.

**My** name is . . .

Victoria    Booth

. . . and if that isn't **your** name then shut this book immediately, you loathsome intruder. How dare you invade my privacy!

If, on the other hand, the name above is the same as yours, then you must be **me**, my dearest friend. Welcome and come inside!

Let's start with Mum and Dad, or Ma and Pa, or Mother and Father, or Mom and Pop. For the next umph number of years you are forced by these bigger, stronger and usually more hairy persons to attend daily that torture emporium known as St Ethel's Education Establishment for Trainee Adults or some such pretentious name. *'SKOOL' to you! This is the place where you 'COULD TRY HARDER', where you seem to show 'LACK OF INTEREST', where 'UNLESS THERE IS AN IMPROVEMENT' . . . you know the rest!

Well, how about them! Mum and Dad can nag you like mad to make yourself worthy of the illustrious family name, to be a credit to all the other highly intelligent geniuses (or is it genii? Oh no, they come out of old lamps) that pervade your learned family, but HOW GOOD AT SCHOOL WERE THEY? It's darned easy for them to pull the wool over your eyes but in the world of other GROWN-UPS (GROANS from now on) how do they rate? Are MUM and DAD really thick as two short planks? COULD THEY DO BETTER? Is there ROOM FOR IMPROVEMENT? Where does their LACK OF INTEREST show? You'll feel a whole lot better about the unequal struggle after you've asked Dad to explain the Theory of Relativity and marked his report accordingly! So get to work; you'll be amazed!

*John Astrop! Your spelling is atroshus.

# TEASERS FOR MUM AND DAD

This set of questions is only for Mum and Dad. You don't have to know the answer. Get them to prove they're right. Bluffing and feeble excuses lose marks. Each question can have a maximum of 10 marks. Be ruthless.

| SUBJECT | MUM'S MARKS | DAD'S MARKS |
|---|---|---|
| **ENGLISH** | | |
| What is the past participle of the verb to dive? | $\frac{9}{10}$ | |
| Spell the following: RHYTHM CHRYSANTHEMUM PHARMACEUTICAL | | $\frac{5}{10}$ |
| **MATHS** | | |
| What is one third of a quarter of three quarters? | $\frac{10}{10}$ | 10 |
| What is 5 in binary maths? | | $\frac{9}{10}$ |
| **HISTORY** | | |
| Ask for any three dates from the anniversaries at the back of this book. | $\frac{0}{10}$ | $\frac{0}{10}$ |

| SUBJECT | MUM'S MARKS | DAD'S MARKS |
|---|---|---|
| **GEOGRAPHY** | | |
| Where and what are the:<br>APPENINES<br>APPALACHIANS<br>URALS | | $9\frac{3}{4}/10$ |
| **SCIENCE** | | |
| What are the following:<br>$CO_2$<br>$H_2SO_4$<br>$H_2O$ | $10/10$ | |
| Explain briefly Einstein's Theory of Relativity. | | $0/10$ |
| **MUSIC** | | |
| What is the current No. 1 in the U.K. charts? | $0/10$ | |
| Sing it! | $0/10$ | |

# MUM'S ART

## Mum draw Dad

# DAD'S ART

## Dad draw Mum

# MUM'S ANNUAL REPORT

Base this on general work over the year. Look back at how helpful or mystified Mama was when you needed help with the vast amounts of unreasonable homework your torturers gave you. Look at the grades on the opposite page and award the appropriate merits for Mum's abilities.

| SUBJECT | GRADE | COMMENTS |
|---|---|---|
| ENGLISH | A | |
| | | |
| MATHS | C | |
| | | |
| HISTORY | B + | |
| | | |
| GEOGRAPHY | A - | |
| | | |
| SCIENCE | A | |
| | | |
| MUSIC | A | |
| | | |
| ART | A | |
| | | |

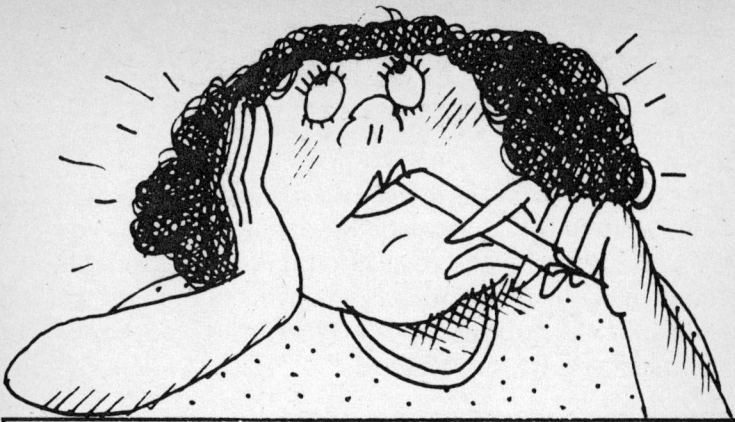

## GRADES

| | |
|---|---|
| A+ | No question. Mum's a genius. |
| A | Not quite a genius but pretty darned good! |
| A− | Helps with my homework and GETS IT RIGHT! |
| B+ | Helps with my homework and often gets it right. |
| B | Helps with my homework. |
| B− | Tries to help, etc. |
| C+ | Doesn't think it's good for me to be helped. |
| C | We never did it like that, darling! |
| C− | Oh, I forgot all that stuff when I left school! |
| D | Better ask Dad! |
| E | Must have inherited my brilliance from Granny. |

# DAD'S ANNUAL REPORT

OK, now go through the same procedure for Papa and award the appropriate merits for his abilities.

| SUBJECT | GRADE | COMMENTS |
|---|---|---|
| ENGLISH | A - | |
| | | |
| MATHS | A | |
| | | |
| HISTORY | | |
| | | |
| GEOGRAPHY | | |
| | | |
| SCIENCE | | |
| | | |
| MUSIC | | |
| | | |
| ART | | |
| | | |

# GRADES

| | |
|---|---|
| A+ | No question. He's a genius. |
| A | Not quite a genius but hard to live up to. |
| A− | Helps with my homework and GETS IT RIGHT! |
| B+ | Helps with my homework and OFTEN gets it right. |
| B | Helps with my homework. |
| B− | Tries to help but . . . |
| C+ | Doesn't think it's good for me to be helped. |
| C | It would only confuse me if I did it his way! |
| C− | He's had a very hard day at work. |
| D | Better ask Mum! |
| E | Must have inherited brilliance from Grandpa! |

# GROANS

Dictionary definition:
GROAN – Deep inarticulate sound expressing pain, grief or disapproval.

Our definition:
GROAN – Groan-up or adolt*

Make no mistake, the GROANS are a permanent fixture in your life and their sole objective is to TURN YOU INTO ONE OF THEM!

HOW, you may say (and I'm glad you did), HOW can we avoid this disaster?

Well, first of all we'll have to be able to tell the difference between GROANS and OTHERS.

Try this check-list and see how many you know.

*Watch the spelling again, Astrop! Your Groanfather would be ashamed of you.

# GROANS

1. Think you are less intelligent than they are and if you follow their magnificent example you will probably become more intelligent as you get older.

2. Say things to you that they would never dare to say to someone their own size.

3. Take away things that belong to you in order to punish you.

4. Hit you.

5. Ignore you.

6. Force you to perform for their friends.

7. Compare you with others. You know, 'Why can't you be like . . .'

8. Choose for you. Everything. (On the basis that everything that you like is BAD FOR YOU or LOOKS TERRIBLE or is RUBBISH.)

GROAN . . . GROAN . . . GROAN . . .

# GROAN POWER

What GROANS say and do can make you mad. These irritations are usually based on the idea that you're hopeless, helpless and hapless until you become a GROAN-UP like them. Keep a record of their beastly bullyings for the long-awaited moment when YOU tower above THEM!

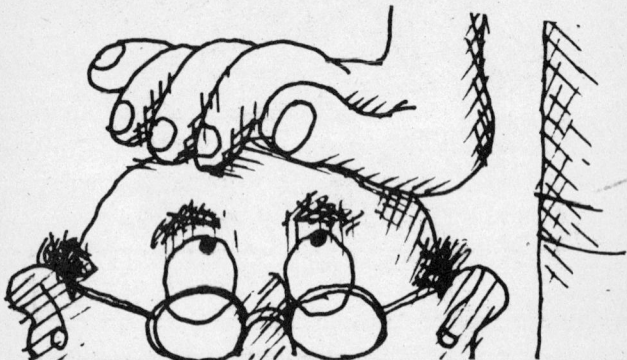

The shopkeeper serves the GROAN behind you. Are you invisible?

A cheerful GROAN pats you on the head (Woof! Woof!).

A non-cheerful GROAN pats you somewhere else (harder!).

The waiter didn't give you a menu. Thinks Mum and Dad will decide for you.

They're talking about you as if you weren't there (Does he/she like cabbage?).

You get an early, burnt, rushed, fishfinger supper before their friends come round for paella and pro-fiteroles.

You get to finish up everything next day, slightly soggy, and all the interesting bits have gone.

# GROAN SPOTTING

A quick reference to some familiar GROANS. Any of these silhouettes on the horizon is an excuse to retreat with great speed. Avoidance is your best weapon. Use the check-list to indicate your success or failure rate.

THUMPER

FUG

HUGGER

YACKETY YAK

KISSER

PRODDER

TICKLER

| Put a tick in the appropriate column. | | |
|---|---|---|
| GROAN-TYPE | AVOIDED | WAS CAUGHT |
| THE PRODDER | | |
| THE TICKLER | | |
| YACKETY-YAK | | |
| THE KISSER | | |
| THE THUMPER | | |
| THE PINCHER | | |
| THE HUGGER | | |
| THE FUG | | |

# PINK FOR A GIRL
# BLUE FOR A BOY

In the olden days men found it almost impossible to boil an egg and women practically fainted if they had to mend a fuse. But in this enlightened age all is different. Or is it? Can it be that you live with a couple of chauvinists? Award CPs (chauvinist points) as indicated.

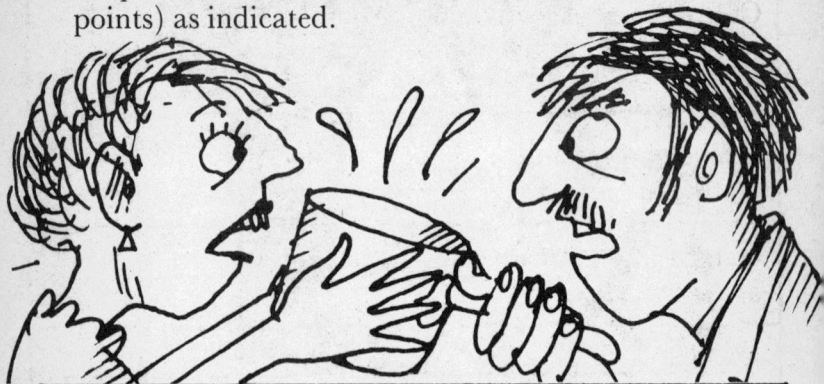

|  | MUM | DAD |
|---|---|---|
| Does Dad go out to work, come home late, expect his supper to be ready on the table, eat it and watch TV for the rest of the evening while Mum washes up and does the ironing? If yes, give them both 50 CPs. |  |  |
| Does Mum go out to work, come home late, expect her supper to be ready on the table, eat it and watch TV for the rest of the evening while Dad washes up and does the ironing? If yes, give them both 50 CPs. |  |  |

| | MUM | DAD |
|---|---|---|
| Does Mum drive the car? Yes −10. No +10. | −10 | −10 |
| Does Dad ever use the washing-machine? Yes −10. No +10. | −10 | −10 |
| Can Dad cook, unaided, a Sunday roast with all the trimmings? Yes −10. No +10. | −10 | +10 |
| Can Mum, unaided, change a wheel on the car? Yes −10. No +10. | +10 | −10 |
| Can Mum deal with a fuse or change an electrical plug? Yes −10. No +10. | −10 | −10 |
| Are they Mum's saucepans and Dad's tools? Yes +10 each. No −10 each. | +10 | +10 |
| Does Dad ever make the bed? Yes −10. No +10. | −10 | −10 |
| Does Mum ever do decorating? Yes −10. No +10. | −10 | +10 |
| Does Dad ever do the household shopping with his own shopping-list? Yes −10. No +10. | −10 | +10 |
| TOTAL | | |

Highest scorer is a chauvinist.
Lowest scorer is a chauvinist's assistant.

# IN AND OUT

Things change, and what you and your friends liked last year seem a bit old hat this year. Things which your crowd think are OK are filled IN IN the IN column and things which are really corny are written OUT IN the OUT column. Let's hope this year, filling IN isn't OUT!

| IN | OUT |
|----|-----|
|    |     |
|    |     |
|    |     |
|    |     |
|    |     |

| IN | OUT |
|---|---|
| CLOTHES | |
| | |
| | |
| | |
| | |
| | |

| IN | OUT |
|---|---|
| **TEACHER** | |
| Miss Hewlett | Miss Tayler |
| **SUBJECT** | |
| Maths | science |
| **SPORT** | |
| Gym | Netbal |
| **DRINK** | |
| Lemon | Apple juce |
| **TV PROGRAMME** | |
| Silas | Play skool |

| IN | OUT |
|---|---|
| POP GROUP | |
| | |
| MALE SINGER | |
| | |
| FEMALE SINGER | |
| | |
| PHRASE MEANING GOOD | |
| | |
| PHRASE MEANING BAD | |
| | |

# WICKED DREAMS

The people I'd most like to splat a custard pie in the face of . . .

Miss Tayler

Miss Lee

The pompous twits I'd most like to put a whoopee cushion under . . .

If I could give my teachers 10,000 lines they would write 'I must not . . .

give my pupils homework
because homework rotts the brain

The greedy hogs I'd most like to give a hot mustard éclair to are . . .

The places I'd most like to put a double-strength stink-bomb would be . . .

The cages I'd most like to leave open at the nearest
zoo are . . .

The laws of the land I'd most like to break (and get away with it) are . . .

The place I'd most like to be a fly on the wall is . . .

# SECRET NAMES

Pseudonyms or pen-names have been used for centuries by authors who didn't want their friends to know they'd been writing such dreary and boring books – much the same as aliases used by criminals. Actors, of course, not only use stage names, they usually disguise themselves as well, in order to keep their identity a secret. It's obviously going to be very useful to have a few of these names of your own for the moments when you want to say it wasn't me, it was —.

A good way to start is to take your own name and shuffle it. For eggsarmful:

JOHN ASTROP reshuffled will make
JOHAN PROST
JOOP STRAHN
JOSH PARTON etc.

OK, who said it also makes HARPO J SNOT? Go and do your own.

Try using Scrabble letters or cut up squares of paper to make it easy. Don't stop at yourself; create secret names for all the family.

| REAL NAME | SECRET NAME |
|-----------|-------------|
|           |             |
|           |             |
|           |             |
|           |             |
|           |             |
|           |             |
|           |             |
|           |             |
|           |             |
|           |             |
|           |             |
|           |             |
|           |             |
|           |             |
|           |             |

# AUTOGRAPHS OF
# MY FAVOURITE PEOPLE

# THE BIG
# HANDWRITING
# GIVE-AWAY

What your favourite people are REALLY like as shown by the famous handwriting expert, YOU.

Below are a few good guides to understanding people's characters from their spidery scrawls.

# WEIGHT

| | |
|---|---|
| **HEAVY** | Easy-going, pleasure-loving. In fact, a lovable clod. |

*Good luck*

| | |
|---|---|
| **MEDIUM** | Likes work and pleasure equally. When you want to play, they want to work. |

*See you when I've*

| | |
|---|---|
| **SKINNY** | Refined, sensitive, loves work. Has to be nuts! |

*I have twenty more to get*

# SIZE

| LARGE | Proud, generous, frank and a blooming old show-off. |
|---|---|

*How are you?*

| MEDIUM | Well-balanced, even-tempered and rather boring. |
|---|---|

*I'm looking forward.*

| SMALL | Cheerful, strong opinions, thrifty, and a right old know-it-all. |
|---|---|

*If you get a chance can you*

| TINY | Neat, fussy, pernickety and a bit of an old Scrooge. |
|---|---|

*No I don't want to let you have a copy of my*

# SHAPE

| SPIKY | A sharp mind, firm, with a temper like a time-bomb. |
|---|---|

*I shall be furious!*

| ROUNDED | Good-tempered, kind-hearted, artistic, cuddly slob. |
|---|---|

*do come round*

| CURLY | Imaginative and self-important, exaggerates to get attention. |
|---|---|

*Copper coloured*

| NARROW | Holds in feelings, not very good at letting go. |
|---|---|

*I can't tell you what*

| BROAD | Strong character, very independent. A great dictator. |
|---|---|

*OK for now !*

# SLOPE

| FORWARD | Sensitive, tender-hearted, affectionate. Easily conned. |
|---------|--------------------------------------------------------|

*I like other people very*

| UPRIGHT | Self-controlled, honest, but likely to put a foot in it. |
|---------|----------------------------------------------------------|

*is a bit thick and*

| BACK-WARD | Original, obstinate and really enjoys being awkward for the sake of it. |
|-----------|------------------------------------------------------------------------|

*I don't want to do the*

| ALL WAYS | Nervy, unsettled, changeable. Not good at making decisions. Or are they? Not sure . . . |
|----------|----------------------------------------------------------------------------------------|

*Still perhaps I could even*

# CAPITAL LETTERS

| PLAIN | Simple, clear-headed, confident. Maddeningly efficient! |
|---|---|

*Come to a Party*

| SCROLLY | Affected, vain, desire for importance. Play-acting again! |
|---|---|

*Come to a Party*

| STRANGE | Imaginative, original. Probably a genius or a looney! |
|---|---|

*Come to a Party*

| TALL | Ambitious, confident. A treader on other people's toes on the road to success! |
|---|---|

*Come to a Party*

| SHORT | Unambitious, modest. A good person to share cake with. |
|---|---|

*Come to a Party*

# CROSSING Ts

| | |
|---|---|
| | |
| Obstinate | Idealistic |
| | |
| Determined | Imaginative |
| | |
| Impatient | Irresponsible |
| | |
| Aggressive | Good-humoured |

# DOTTING Is

| | |
|---|---|
| Good memory | *i* |
| Imaginative | *i* |
| Optimistic | *i* |
| Attention-seeking | *i* |
| Cautious | *i* |

I must write my own lines
I must write my own lines
I must write my own lines
**I must write my own lines**
I must write my own lines
I must write my own lines
I must write my own lines
I must write my own lines
must write my own lines
write my own lines

# OPINIONS

These pages are about what I think and about what I think you think and about what I think you think I think about what you think . . . no, wait a minute . . . I think . . .

# I THINK

God is . . . *very nice*

Politics are . . . *annoying*

The bomb is . . .

Love is . . . *Lovely*

School is . . . *Sometimes nice*

Music is . . . *fun*

Violence is . . . *horrid*

Life is . . . *quite nice*

Death is . . . *awful*

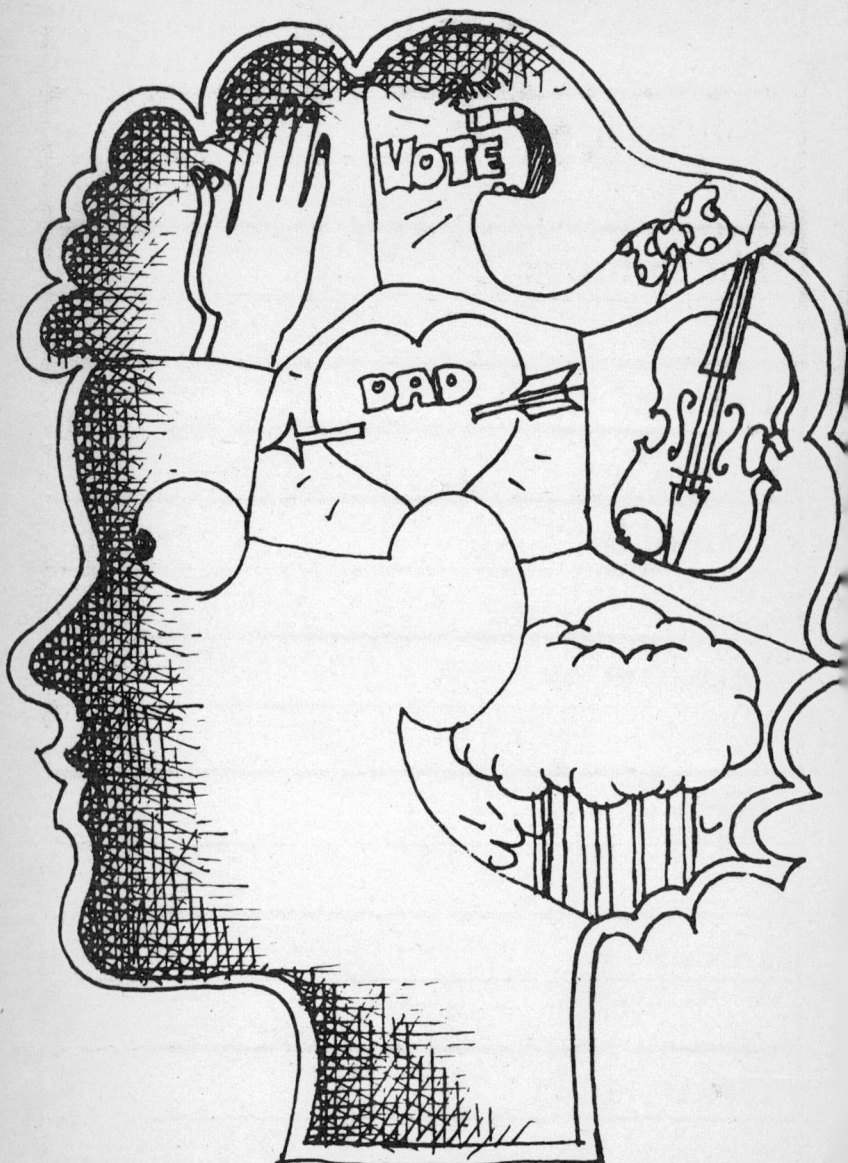

## MUM THINKS (I think)

God is . . . *Good*

Politics are . . . *O.k.*

The bomb is . . .

Love is . . . *Lovely*

School is . . . *Good for you*

Music is . . . *peaceful*

Violence is . . . *horrid*

Life is . . . *nice*

Death is . . . *horrid*

## **DAD THINKS** (I think)

God is . . . not true

Politics are . . . a newsenee

The bomb is . . .

Love is . . . lovely

School is . . . very good for you

Music is . . . nice!

Violence is . . . hottid

Life is . . . a bore

Death is . . . hotrid !

# DISGUSTING HABITS DISCUSSED

The world of secrets contains many dark shadows. Is it hard to imagine Dad as a perpetual nose gardener, a 'stop picking that scab or it'll never get better' athlete? Did Mum actually nibble her talons down to the elbow in frenzies of school excitement? Did they really do these dreadful deeds? OF COURSE THEY DID! AND DO!

Every time they give you that old lecture, you can bring out your 'PARENTAL DISGUSTING HABIT CHECK-LIST' to bear witness to their ghastly hypocrisy.

Train your beady eyes to be like theirs, spot the moments when they think they are unobserved and tick the check-list for later use.

| DEED | MUM | DAD |
|------|-----|-----|
| NOSE-PICKING | | |
| NAIL-NIBBLING | | ✓ |
| EATING WITHOUT WASHING HANDS FIRST | some times | |
| LEAVING SMELLY CLOTHES ABOUT | | ✓ |

| DEED | DAD | MUM |
|---|---|---|
| SPEAKING WITH THE MOUTH FULL | | |
| PICKING TEETH INDISCREETLY | √ a bit | |
| EAR-WAX MINING | | √ |

| DEED | MUM | DAD |
|---|---|---|
| SMOKING LIKE A CHIMNEY | | |
| BURPING | ✓ | |
| LETTING POLLY OUT OF THE CAGE | | |

# HANDY INFORMATION

Verify your belief that you are surrounded by misers, looneys, bullies and sex maniacs. All their deep secrets are revealed by careful study of the dirty little puddy. What a tale those hands can tell!

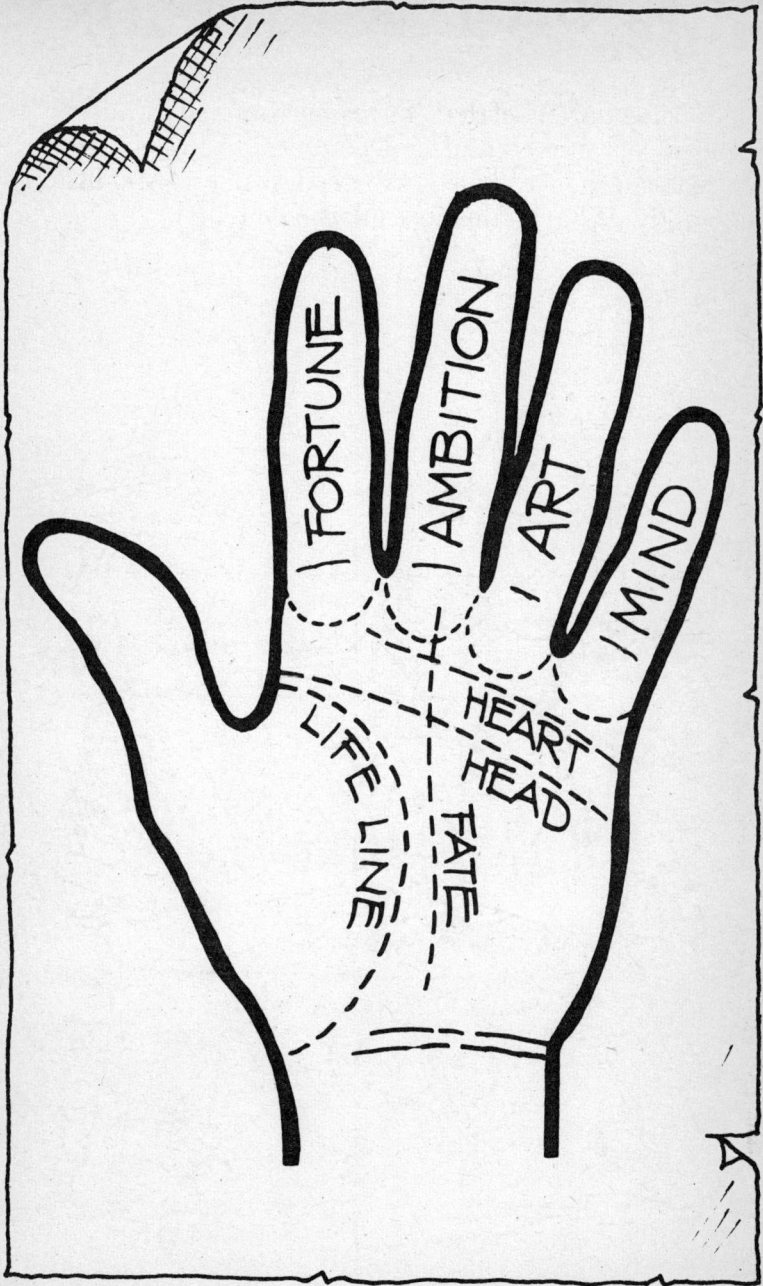

# LIFE LINE

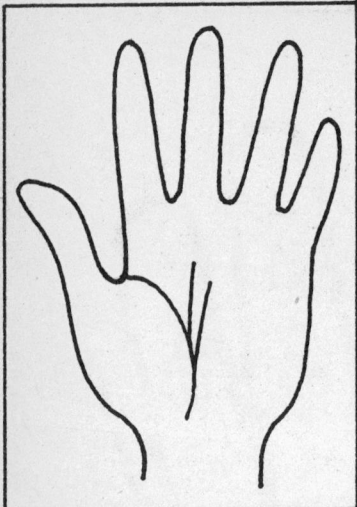

Very ambitious

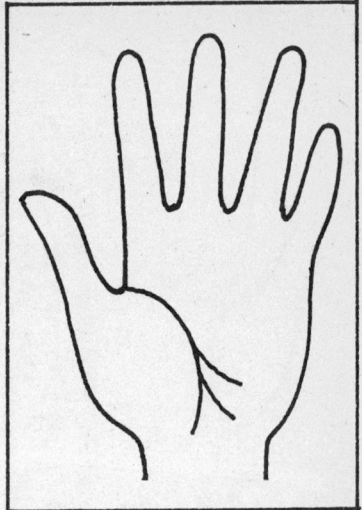

A great traveller

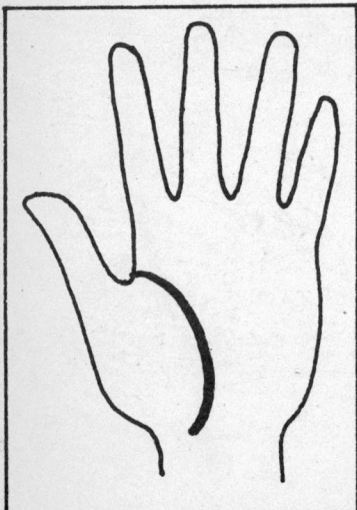

Bursting with health

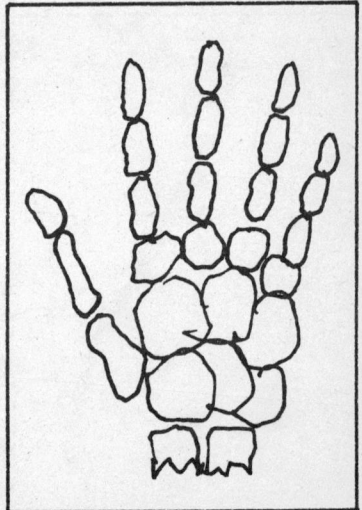

DEAD!

# LIFE LINE

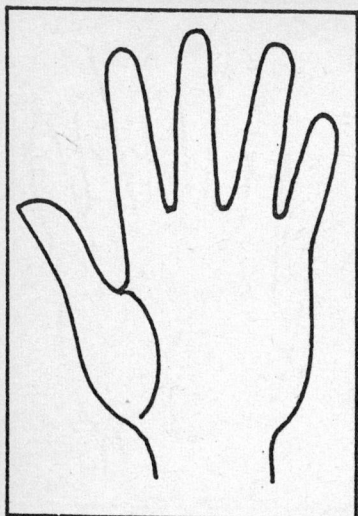

A great stayer-at-home

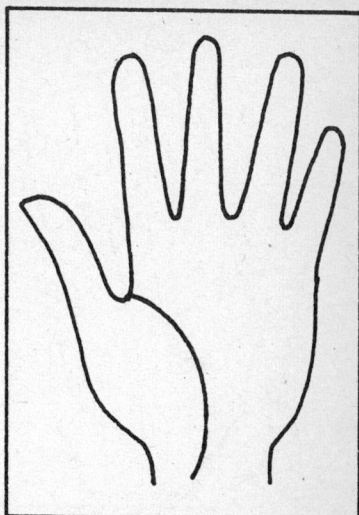

Long liver

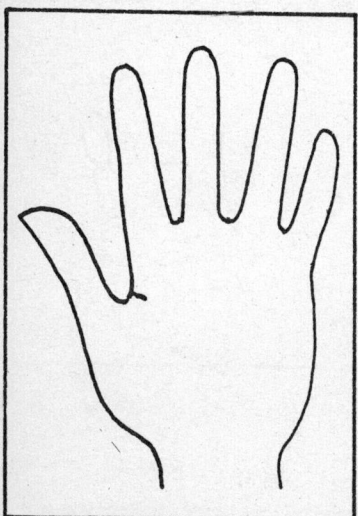

Short liver

Liver and bacon

# FATE LINE

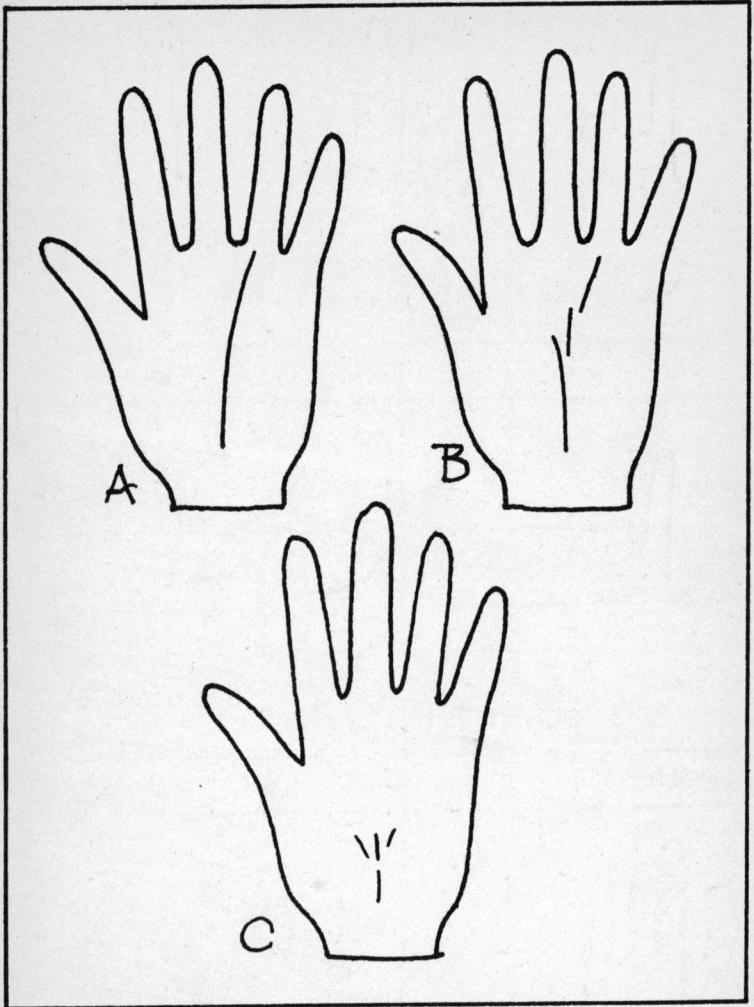

A   Achiever, will reach the top early.

B   After a struggle will eventually be successful.

C   Cultivate a sympathetic bank manager.

# HEART LINE

| | | |
|---|---|---|
| Very loving | Flirty | Dirty |
| Hearty | Arty | Frigid |
| Rigid | | |

# HEAD LINE

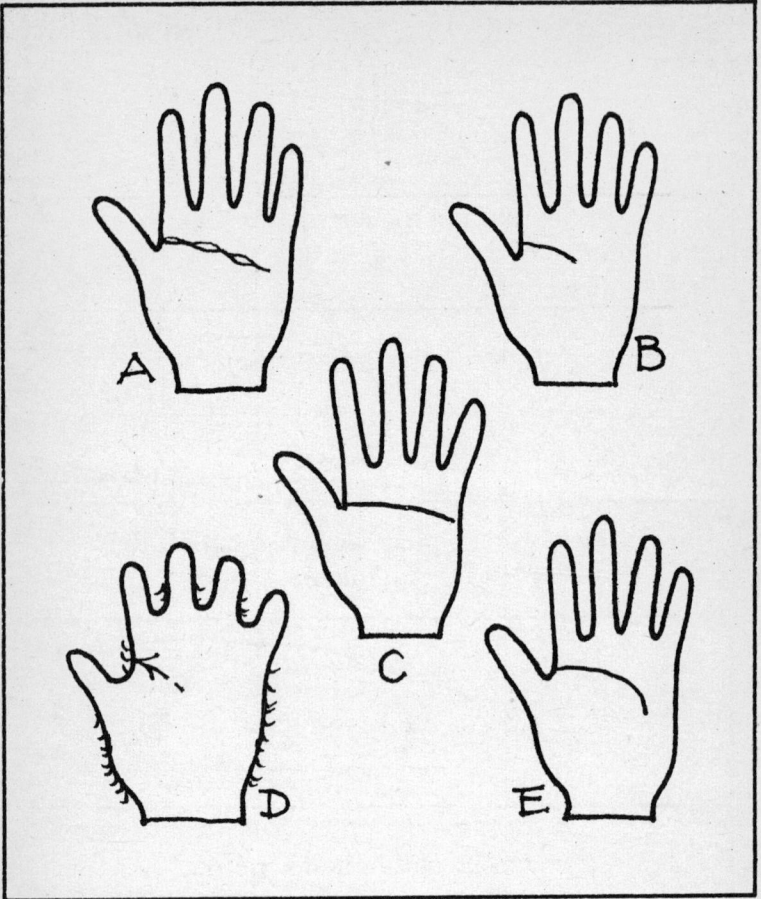

A  Timid, over-sensitive, a shrinking violet. A bit clinging.

B  Slow starter. Not the brightest thinker but gets there in the end.

C  Intellectual. A really great mind.

D  Neanderthal. A really good friend.

E  Independent and reckless, in fact a clever old looney.

# NAILS

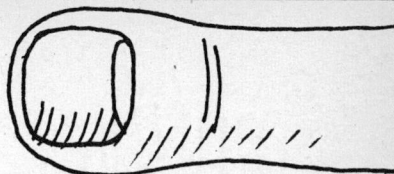

Frank, but not too energetic. Not a good judge of things. Could be an embarrassment.

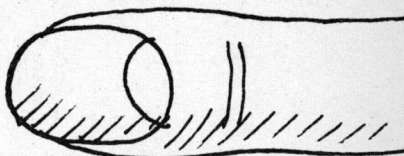

Sweet-tempered, peace at any price. Lets you get away with masses.

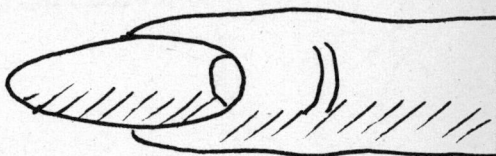

Lethal within half a metre.

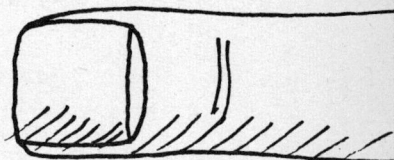

Don't get into an argument with this one. It'll go on and on and on and . . .

# FINGER SHAPES

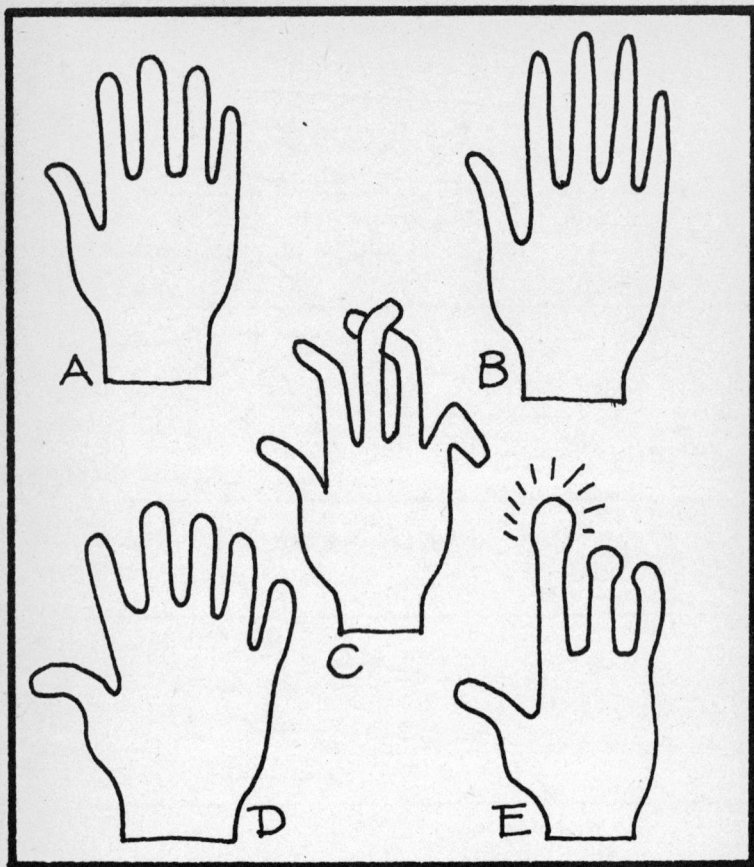

A Comfort-loving, careless and lazy. Temperamental and moody.

B Realistic, punctual, down to earth. A real old stick-in-the-mud.

C Broken!

D Unsettled, unconventional, outdoor type. Can be sudden with the heavy hand.

E Stop messing about. This is E.T.!

DRAW YOUR OWN HAND HERE

# FIWERNT AND
# WANNABY

This one's easy. Everybody knows you are the best possible with the greatest potential, the most magnificent and the most unbelievably indescribable, but try this on yourself and those near and dear. FIWERNT me who would I WANNABY?

| FIWERNT (Name) | I'd WANNABY |
|---|---|
| | |
| | |
| | |
| | |
| | |
| | |
| | |
| | |
| | |
| | |
| | |
| | |
| | |
| | |
| | |
| | |
| | |
| | |

# HAPPY ANNIVERSARY*

When caught with that forbidden bag of toof-rotting toffee-chews how great to be able to say, 'I was just quietly celebrating the 90th anniversary of the death of the inventor of the saxophone!' When asked at school why you have failed to finish the previous night's homework, you answer, 'But Miss, we were observing the 117th anniversary of the taking out of the first patent on barbed wire! It was a real family get-together.'

This fund of things to celebrate for each day of the year was put together with much research, falling asleep with sheer boredom and unlimited inaccuracy. Cherish it, brighten a glum day, and celebrate.

*All anniversaries are calculated on fingers and toes for the year 1984.

# JANUARY

1. 84th anniversary of the start of the 20th century.

2. 83rd anniversary of the opening of the first municipal crematorium.

3. 114th anniversary of the start of building the Brooklyn Bridge.

4. 118th anniversary of the discovery of Asteroid 86.

5. 507th anniversary of the death of Charles the Bold.

6. 72nd anniversary of New Mexico becoming the 47th U.S. state.

7. 534th anniversary of the founding of Glasgow University.

8. 44th anniversary of sugar rationing in Britain.

9. 13th anniversary of Clive Dunn's 'Grandad' topping the U.K. charts.

10. 26th anniversary of 'Great Balls of Fire' topping the U.K. charts.

11. 120th anniversary of the opening of Charing Cross Station.

12. 109th anniversary of Kwang-su being made Emperor of China.

13. 109th anniversary of the discovery of Asteroid 141.

14. 126th anniversary of the attempted assassination of Napoleon III.

15. 107th anniversary of the collapse of the Dover–Folkestone tunnel.

16. 52nd anniversary of the recording of Duke Ellington's 'It don't mean a thing'.

17. 101st anniversary of the defeat of U.S. troops by Captain Jack and the Modoc Indians.

18. 73rd anniversary of the first landing of a plane on a ship.

19. 199th anniversary of the first balloon ascent in Ireland.

20. 179th anniversary of the opening of London Docks.

21. 42nd anniversary of the first recording of 'One o'Clock Jump'.

22. 60th anniversary of the resignation of Prime Minister Stanley Baldwin.

23. 60th anniversary of the formation of the first British Labour Government.

24. 6th anniversary of a Russian satellite crashing to earth at Yellowknife, Canada.

25. 125th anniversary of the death of William Wordsworth's sister.

26. 79th anniversary of the discovery of the world's largest diamond.

27. 5th anniversary of Ian Dury's 'Hit Me with Your Rhythm Stick' topping the U.K. charts.

28. 155th anniversary of the execution of 'body-snatcher' William Burke.

29. 136th anniversary of the Scots adopting Greenwich Mean Time.

30. 67th anniversary of the first recordings of the Original Dixieland Jazz Band.

31. 378th anniversary of the execution of Guy Fawkes.

# FEBRUARY

1. 60th anniversary of the recognition of the U.S.S.R. by the British government.

2. 67th anniversary of bread rationing in Britain in War I.

3. 5th anniversary of Blondie's 'Heart of Glass' topping the U.K. charts.

4. 22nd anniversary of the first *Sunday Times* colour supplement.

5. 202nd anniversary of Minorca being captured from the British by the Spanish.

6. 10th anniversary of the independence of Grenada.

7. 90th anniversary of the death of Adolph Sax, inventor of the saxophone.

8. 397th anniversary of the beheading of Mary Queen of Scots.

9. 42nd anniversary of the beginning of soap rationing in Britain during World War II.

10. 144th anniversary of Queen Victoria's wedding day.

11. 126th anniversary of the vision of the Virgin Mary appearing to three young girls at Lourdes.

12. 107th anniversary of the first public demonstration of the telephone.

13. 292nd anniversary of the massacre of the Macdonalds at Glencoe, Scotland.

14. 92nd anniversary of a fall of scarlet worms after a snowstorm in Massachusetts.

15. 102nd anniversary of the first shipment of frozen meat from New Zealand to Britain.

16. 61st anniversary of the opening of Tutankhamen's tomb.

17. 75th anniversary of the death of Geronimo, Apache chief.

18. 54th anniversary of the discovery of the planet Pluto.

19. 107th anniversary of Edison taking out a patent on the first gramophone.

20. 123rd anniversary of the steeple of Chichester Cathedral being blown off in a great storm.

21. 548th anniversary of the murder of James I of Scotland.

22. 10th anniversary of the recognition of independence for Bangladesh by Pakistan.

23. 121st anniversary of the announcement of the discovery of the source of the River Nile.

24. 38th anniversary of the election of Juan Perón as President of Argentina.

25. 677th anniversary of the coronation of Edward II of England.

26. 187th anniversary of the issue of one-pound banknotes in England.

27. 427th anniversary of the opening of the first Russian Embassy in London.

28. 115th anniversary of the death of the French poet and statesman, Lamartine.

29. 104th anniversary of the completion of the cutting of the St Gothard tunnel.

# MARCH

1. 173rd anniversary of the massacre of the Mame-lukes by Mehemet Ali in Egypt.

2. 102nd anniversary of the attempted assassina-tion of Queen Victoria.

3. 139th anniversary of Florida becoming the 27th U.S. state.

4. 123rd anniversary of the discovery of Angelina (Asteroid 64).

5. 114th anniversary of the completion of the Bombay to Calcutta railway.

6. 156th anniversary of the death of Hongi Hika, Ngapuhi War Chief of New Zealand.

7. 191st anniversary of the declaration of war on Spain by France.

8. 282nd anniversary of the accession of Queen Anne of Great Britain.

9. 188th anniversary of Napoleon's marriage to Josephine.

10. 10th anniversary of the last person finding out that World War II had ended (1974!).

11. 19th anniversary of Tom Jones's 'It's Not Unusual' topping the U.K. charts.

12. 54th anniversary of the beginning of Gandhi's campaign of civil disobedience.

13. 203rd anniversary of the discovery of the planet Uranus.

14. 101st anniversary of the death of Karl Marx.

15. 2028th anniversary of the assassination of Julius Caesar in Rome.

16. 58th anniversary of the first successful launching of a liquid-fuelled rocket.

17. 208th anniversary of the forcing of the British to evacuate Boston.

18. 115th anniversary of the founding of the synagogue in Great Portland Street, London.

19. 26th anniversary of the opening of the London Planetarium.

20. 165th anniversary of the opening of Burlington Arcade, London.

21. 571st anniversary of the accession of Henry V of England.

22. 89th anniversary of the first demonstration of a cinematograph film.

23. 232nd anniversary of the first known example of printing in Canada.

24. 60th anniversary of Greece becoming a republic.

25. 185th anniversary of the occupation of Tuscany by the French.

26. 125th anniversary of the first sighting of the supposed planet Vulcan.

27. 130th anniversary of the declaration of war against Russia by France.

28. 106th anniversary of the installation of electric lights at Westminster Palace.

29. 113th anniversary of the opening of the Royal Albert Hall, London.

30. 117th anniversary of Russia's sale of Alaska to the Americans.

31. 95th anniversary of the inauguration of the Eiffel Tower, Paris.

# APRIL

1. 93rd anniversary of the official opening of the London–Paris telephone line.

2. 112th anniversary of the death of the inventor of the Morse Code.

3. 927th anniversary of the accession of Malcolm III of Scotland.

4. 403rd anniversary of Francis Drake being knighted.

5. 131st anniversary of the discovery of Themis (Asteroid 24).

6. 98th anniversary of the founding of Vancouver.

7. 245th anniversary of the execution of Dick Turpin, highwayman.

8. 45th anniversary of the abdication of King Zog of Albania.

9. 56th anniversary of Turkey ceasing to recognize Islam as the state religion.

10. 164th anniversary of the first British settlers in South Africa.

11. 295th anniversary of the coronation of William III and Mary II of England.

12. 123rd anniversary of the beginning of the bombardment of Fort Sumter.

13. 1170th anniversary of the death of King Krum of Bulgaria.

14. 513th anniversary of the last day of the Battle of Barnet.

15. 72nd anniversary of the sinking of the 'Titanic'.

16. 118th anniversary of the attempted assassination of Czar Alexander II of Russia.

17. 31st anniversary of 'How Much Is That Doggie in the Window' reaching No. 1 in the charts.

18. 110th anniversary of the discovery and naming of Coggia's Comet by M. Coggia.

19. 205th anniversary of the beginning of the American War of Independence.

20. 72nd anniversary of the death of Bram Stoker, author of *Dracula*.

21. 120th anniversary of Garibaldi receiving the freedom of London.

22. 970th anniversary of the day before the defeat of the Danes at Clontarf, Ireland.

23. 368th anniversary of the death of William Shakespeare.

24. 14th anniversary of the first Chinese earth-orbiting satellite.

25. 20th anniversary of the stealing of the head of the Little Mermaid statue in Copenhagen.

26. 115th anniversary of the shooting of Abraham Lincoln's assassin.

27. 34th anniversary of the recognition of the state of Israel by Britain.

28. 214th anniversary of Captain Cook's landing in Botany Bay.

29. 555th anniversary of the ending of the siege of Orléans.

30. 555th anniversary of the day after the ending of the siege of Orléans.

# MAY

1. 144th anniversary of the first 'Penny Black' postage stamp being made public.

2. 19th anniversary of the first satellite television transmission.

3. 143rd anniversary of the day New Zealand was proclaimed a British colony.

4. 141st anniversary of the day Natal was proclaimed a British colony.

5. 123rd anniversary of H. Goldschmidt's discovery of Panopoea (Asteroid 70).

6. 102nd anniversary of the U.S. ten-year ban on Chinese immigrants.

7. 69th anniversary of the sinking of the 'Lusitania'.

8. 39th anniversary of V.E. day (Victory in Europe).

9. 110th anniversary of the opening of the Victoria Embankment, London.

10. 35th anniversary of the last day that Thailand was called Siam.

11. 298th anniversary of the death of Otto von Guericke, discoverer of the air-pump.

12. 58th anniversary of the end of the British General Strike.

13. 416th anniversary of Queen Mary of Scotland's defeat at the battle of Langside.

14. 11th anniversary of the launch of the Skylab space station.

15. 188th anniversary of Napoleon's entry into Milan.

16. 55th anniversary of the first presentation of the Academy Awards.

17. 94th anniversary of the first regular comic – *Comic Cuts*.

18. 396th anniversary of the first day before the Spanish Armada set sail from Lisbon.

19. 89th anniversary of the release of Oscar Wilde from Pentonville prison.

20. 185th anniversary of the abandoning of the siege of Acre by Napoleon.

21. 90th anniversary of the opening of the Manchester Ship Canal.

22. 12th anniversary of the change of Ceylon's name to Sri Lanka.

23. 283rd anniversary of the execution of Captain Kidd for piracy.

24. 101st anniversary of the opening of the Brooklyn Bridge.

25. 22nd anniversary of 'Nut Rocker' losing its place at the top of the U.K. charts.

26. 116th anniversary of the last public execution in England.

27. 166th anniversary of the birthday of Amelia Bloomer, who gave her name to 'bloomers'.

28. 103rd anniversary of a fall of tons of periwinkles from the sky in Worcester.

29. 100th anniversary of the opening of the steam cable tramway at Highgate, London.

30. 25th anniversary of the first hovercraft flight.

31. 93rd anniversary of the beginning of the Siberian Railway.

# JUNE

1. 69th anniversary of the first attack on London by Zeppelins.

2. 18th anniversary of U.S. Surveyor II's soft landing on the moon.

3. 32nd anniversary of the day after Queen Elizabeth II's coronation.

4. 200th anniversary of the ascent of a female French opera singer in a hot air balloon.

5. 178th anniversary of Louis Napoleon becoming King of Holland.

6. 68th anniversary of the beginning of the Arab revolt in Hejaz.

7. 63rd anniversary of the first sitting of Northern Ireland's parliament.

8. 942nd anniversary of the death of Hardecanute, King of Denmark and England.

9. 2037th anniversary of Crassus's defeat by the Parthians.

10. 57th anniversary of the recording of Jelly Roll Morton's 'The Pearls'.

11. 726th anniversary of the assembling of the 'Mad' parliament in London.

12. 112th anniversary of the opening of the first Japanese railway.

13. 142nd anniversary of Queen Victoria's first train ride.

14. 18th anniversary of the abolition by the Vatican of the *Index to Prohibited Books*.

15. 769th anniversary of King John signing the Magna Carta.

16. 330th anniversary of the abdication of Queen Christina of Sweden.

17. 555th anniversary of the day before the defeat of the English by Joan of Arc at Patay.

18. 167th anniversary of the opening of Waterloo Bridge in London.

19. 67th anniversary of the renunciation by the British Royal Family of their German titles and names.

20. 89th anniversary of the opening of the Kiel Canal.

21. 71st anniversary of the first parachute descent from a plane by a woman.

22. 2201st anniversary of the defeat of Antiochus III by Ptolemy.

23. 172nd anniversary of the day before Napoleon entered Russia.

24. 670th anniversary of the defeat of the English by Robert the Bruce at Bannockburn.

25. 117th anniversary of the taking out of the first patent on barbed wire.

26. 126th anniversary of the end of the Anglo-Chinese War.

27. 84th anniversary of the opening of the London electric tube railway from Bank to Shepherd's Bush.

28. 27th anniversary of Elvis Presley's 'All Shook Up' entering the British charts.

29. 129th anniversary of the first *Daily Telegraph*.

30. 92nd anniversary of an alleged shower of frogs over Birmingham.

# JULY

1. 112th anniversary of the unveiling of the Albert Memorial in London.

2. 84th anniversary of the first Zeppelin flight.

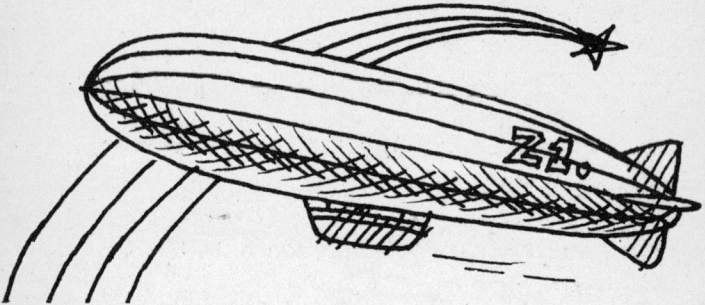

3. 111th anniversary of the discovery of a new comet, Temple.

4. 47th anniversary of the first successful helicopter flight.

5. 167th anniversary of the first issue of sovereigns in Britain.

6. 56th anniversary of the first public showing of a 'talkie' film.

7. 117th anniversary of the discovery of Undina (Asteroid 92).

8. 176th anniversary of the hottest day in London (36.6° centigrade, 99° fahrenheit).

9. 444th anniversary of Henry VIII's divorce from Anne of Cleves.

10. 22nd anniversary of the launching of Telstar 1.

11. 276th anniversary of the Duke of Marlborough's victory at Oudenarde.

12. 793rd anniversary of the taking of Acre by the Crusaders.

13. 28th anniversary of 'Be-Bop-a-Lula' entering the British charts.

14. 25th anniversary of the death of Grock the Clown.

15. 114th anniversary of the coming into force of the National Insurance Act.

16. 39th anniversary of the explosion of the first atomic bomb.

17. 407th anniversary of Martin Frobisher landing at and exploring Baffin Land.

18. 1920th anniversary of the start of the Great Fire of Rome.

19. 15th anniversary of John Fairfax becoming the first man to row across the Atlantic alone.

20. 282nd anniversary of the defeat of the Poles by Charles XII at Clissau.

21. 15th anniversary of Neil Armstrong setting foot on the moon.

22. 130th anniversary of the discovery of Urania (Asteroid 30).

23. 120th anniversary of the return of Dr Livingstone to England.

24. 133rd anniversary of the abolition of British Window Tax.

25. 39th anniversary of the ending of bread rationing in Britain.

26. 1273rd anniversary of the defeat of Roderic at the Battle of Xeres.

27. 9th anniversary of the launching of China's third orbiting satellite.

28. 22nd anniversary of the four-minute failed space flight of Mariner 1.

29. 77th anniversary of the first day of the first Boy Scout Camp.

30. 121st anniversary of the first day in the life of Henry Ford.

31. 486th anniversary of Columbus's discovery of Trinidad.

# AUGUST

1. 252nd anniversary of the laying of the foundation stones of the Bank of England.

2. 95th anniversary of a shower of little toads in Savoy.

3. 173rd anniversary of the birth of the man who was to invent the modern safety lift.

4. 719th anniversary of the defeat of the Barons at Evesham.

5. 100th anniversary of the laying of the cornerstone of the Statue of Liberty.

6. 178th anniversary of the end of the Holy Roman Empire.

7. 126th anniversary of Ottawa becoming the capital of Canada.

8. 21st anniversary of the Great Train Robbery.

9. 1606th anniversary of the Valens defeat by the Gauls at Adrianople.

10. 23rd anniversary of Britain's application for membership of the E.E.C.

11. 107th anniversary of the discovery of the satellites of Mars.

12. 172nd anniversary of the entry of the Duke of Wellington into Madrid.

13. 111th anniversary of the discovery of Franz Josef Land.

14. 96th anniversary of the fall of black rain at the Cape of Good Hope.

15. 70th anniversary of the opening of the Panama Canal.

16. 87th anniversary of the opening of the Tate Gallery in London.

17. 88th anniversary of the first discovery of gold in the Klondike, Canada.

18. 757th anniversary of the death of Genghis Khan.

19. 712th anniversary of the coronation of Edward I.

20. 72nd anniversary of the founder of the Salvation Army, William Booth, joining his Maker.

21. 73rd anniversary of the theft of the 'Mona Lisa' from the Louvre, Paris.

22. 16th anniversary of the first visit of a Pope to South America.

23. 1574th anniversary of Rome being taken by the Visigoths.

24. 1905th anniversary of the destruction of Pompeii by the eruption of Mount Vesuvius.

25. 454th anniversary of the birth of Ivan the Terrible.

26. 2038th anniversary of the landing of Julius Caesar on the coast of Britain.

27. 45th anniversary of the first testing of a turbo-jet engine.

28. 1554th anniversary of the death of St Augustine of Hippo.

29. 31st anniversary of the exploding of the first hydrogen bomb by the Russians.

30. 123rd anniversary of the freeing of slaves in Missouri, U.S.A.

31. 171st anniversary of the start of the siege of San Sebastian.

# SEPTEMBER

1. 105th anniversary of the signing of a peace treaty between Britain and the Zulus.

2. 318th anniversary of the start of the Great Fire of London.

3. 8th anniversary of touchdown on Mars by Viking II.

4. 528th anniversary of the repulse of Mahomet II at Belgrade.

5. 99th anniversary of the first train through the Severn Tunnel, Bristol.

6. 15th anniversary of David Bowie's first entry into the British charts.

7. 136th anniversary of the abolition of serfdom in Austria.

8. 40th anniversary of the landing of a V2 rocket in Britain.

9. 92nd anniversary of the discovery of the fifth satellite of Jupiter.

10. 437th anniversary of the end of the Battle of Pinkey.

11. 275th anniversary of the end of the Battle of Malplaquet.

12. 105th anniversary of the erection of Cleopatra's Needle on the Thames Embankment in London.

13. 72nd anniversary of the beginning of the revolution in San Domingo.

14. 170th anniversary of the composing of 'The Star-Spangled Banner'.

15. 163rd anniversary of Independence Day, Guatemala.

16. 143rd anniversary of the day after Independence Day, San Salvador.

17. 186th anniversary of George Washington's farewell address.

18. 103rd anniversary of the 1881 sighting of Encke's Comet.

19. 127th anniversary of the discovery of Doris and Pales (Asteroids 49 and 50).

20. 18th anniversary of the launching of the 'Queen Elizabeth II'.

21. 81st anniversary of the last total eclipse over the South Pole.

22. 743rd anniversary of the death of Sturluson Snorri, Icelandic poet.

23. 138th anniversary of the discovery of the planet Neptune.

24. 491st anniversary of the day before Columbus set sail on his second expedition.

25. 294th anniversary of the first issue of the first U.S. newspaper.

26. 75th anniversary of the assassination of Prince Ito of Japan.

27. 1495th anniversary of the defeat of Odoacer by Theodoric at Verona.

28. 2474th anniversary of the last day of the Battle of Marathon.

29. 38th anniversary of the fastest knock-out in a boxing match – 10.5 seconds.

30. 25th anniversary of the death of James Dean, star of *Rebel without a Cause*.

# OCTOBER

1. 181st anniversary of the sale of Louisiana to the United States.

2. 114th anniversary of Rome becoming the capital of Italy.

3. Probably the 70th anniversary of the world's first Flag Day.

4. 25th anniversary of the first close-up photographs of the moon.

5. 191st anniversary of the abolition of Christianity by the French.

6. 36th anniversary of Chiang Kai-shek becoming President of China.

7. 412th anniversary of the first celebration of the feast of Our Lady's Rosary.

8. 1108th anniversary of the defeat of Charles the Bald at Andernach.

9. 17th anniversary of the coming into force of the breathalyser test.

10. 14th anniversary of independence for the Fiji Islands.

11. 8th anniversary of the 'Gang of Four' in Peking.

12. 85th anniversary of the beginning of the Anglo–Boer War.

13. 585th anniversary of the coronation of Henry IV of England.

14. 113th anniversary of the observation of Encke's Comet in Britain.

15. 201st anniversary of the first human flight in a balloon.

16. 76th anniversary of the first aeroplane flight in England.

17. 28th anniversary of the opening of the Calder Hall Nuclear Power Station.

18. 158th anniversary of the last lottery to be held in England.

19. 172nd anniversary of the beginning of Napoleon's retreat from Moscow.

20. 11th anniversary of the opening of the Sydney Opera House.

21. 129th anniversary of the rioting in Hyde Park over the cost of bread.

22. 187th anniversary of the first parachute descent from a balloon.

23. 5988th anniversary of the creation of the world, according to Dr John Lightfoot.

24. 336th anniversary of the end of the Thirty Years' War.

25. 337th anniversary of the death of the inventor of the barometer.

26. 26th anniversary of the first transatlantic jet passenger service between New York and Paris.

27. 340th anniversary of the Battle of Newbury.

28. 98th anniversary of the unveiling of the Statue of Liberty.

29. 61st anniversary of Republic Day in Turkey.

30. 162nd anniversary of the completion of the Caledonian Canal.

31. 13th anniversary of an explosion on top of the Post Office Tower in London.

# NOVEMBER

1. 285th anniversary of the founding of the Bank of Scotland.

2. 81st anniversary of the publishing of the first *Daily Mirror*.

3. 56th anniversary of the adoption of the Roman alphabet by the Turks.

4. 375th anniversary of the discovery of the 'Gunpowder Plot'.

5. 144th anniversary of the surrender of Afghanistan to Britain.

6. 32nd anniversary of the exploding of the first U.S. hydrogen bomb.

7. 13th anniversary of Revolution Day in Bangladesh.

8. 10th anniversary of the closing of Covent Garden fruit and vegetable market.

9. 125th anniversary of the abolition of flogging in the British army.

10. 491st anniversary of the discovery of Antigua by Christopher Columbus.

11. 104th anniversary of the hanging of Ned Kelly, Australian outlaw.

12. 197th anniversary of the Great Floods of the River Liffey.

13. 133rd anniversary of the opening of the London–Paris telegraph.

14. 74th anniversary of the first aeroplane take-off from the deck of a ship.

15. 65th anniversary of the taking of Omsk by the Red Army.

16. 234th anniversary of the opening of Westminster Bridge in London.

17. 18th anniversary of the Beach Boys' 'Good Vibrations' becoming the U.K. No. 1.

18. 132nd anniversary of the Duke of Wellington's funeral.

19. 215th anniversary of the opening of Blackfriars Bridge in London.

20. 491st anniversary of the discovery of Puerto Rico.

21. 66th anniversary of the surrender of the German fleet.

22. 266th anniversary of the death of Blackbeard the pirate.

23. 94th anniversary of the separation of Luxembourg from the Netherlands.

24. 345th anniversary of the first observation of the transit of Venus over the Sun.

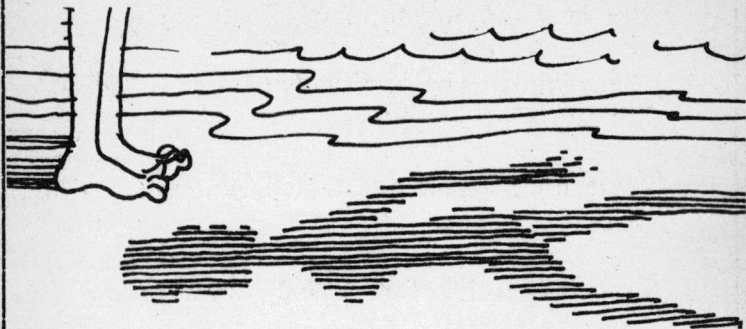

25. 29th anniversary of 'Rock Around the Clock' reaching the top of the U.K. charts.

26. 15th anniversary of the launch of the first French orbiting satellite.

27. 18th anniversary of the opening of the first tidal power station.

28. 26th anniversary of Lord Rockingham's 'Hoots Mon' reaching No. 1 in the U.K. charts.

29. 45th anniversary of the first New Zealand Labour Government.

30. 45th anniversary of the invasion of Finland by the U.S.S.R.

# DECEMBER

1. 63rd anniversary of the first flight of a helium-filled dirigible.

2. 6th anniversary of Rod Stewart's 'Do You Think I'm Sexy' topping the charts.

3. 166th anniversary of Illinois becoming the 21st U.S. state.

4. 186th anniversary of the declaration of war on Naples by France.

5. 51st anniversary of the repeal of Prohibition.

6. 492nd anniversary of the discovery of Haiti.

7. 107th anniversary of the first demonstration of the gramophone by Edison.

8. 120th anniversary of the opening of the Clifton Suspension Bridge, Bristol.

9. 242nd anniversary of the death of Scheele, the discoverer of oxygen.

10. 36th anniversary of Human Rights Day.

11. 296th anniversary of James II's flight from England.

12. 21st anniversary of Independence Day in Kenya.

13. 176th anniversary of Napoleon's capture of Madrid.

14. 73rd anniversary of Amundsen's visit to the South Pole.

15. 94th anniversary of the death of Sitting Bull, Chief of the Sioux.

16. 58th anniversary of the recording of 'Doctor Jazz' by Jelly Roll Morton and his Red Hot Peppers.

17. 68th anniversary of the assassination of Rasputin.

18. 15th anniversary of the abolition of the death penalty in Britain.

19. 43rd anniversary of the British evacuation of Penang.

20. 16th anniversary of Rolf Harris's 'Two Little Boys' topping the hit parade.

21. 47th anniversary of the first showing of Disney's *Snow White and the Seven Dwarfs*.

22. 1st anniversary of the author's most boring day last year.

23. 12th anniversary of 'Long-haired Lover from Liverpool' topping the U.K. charts.

24. 78th anniversary of the world's first public radio broadcast.

25. 125th anniversary of the supposed invention of ice-hockey.

26. 849th anniversary of the accession of King Stephen of England.

27. 4th anniversary of 'There's no one quite like Grandma' topping the U.K. charts.

28. 89th anniversary of the first moving-picture performance (in Paris).

29. 218th anniversary of the birth of waterproofing expert Charles Mackintosh.

30. 90th anniversary of the death of women's rights campaigner Amelia Bloomer.

31. 285th anniversary of the first day of a tax on windows in England.